Soviet Russia's Space Progr... ...tory and Legacy of ...n

By Charles River Editors

Alex Zelenko's picture of an R-7 rocket used by the Soviets

About Charles River Editors

Charles River Editors provides superior editing and original writing services across the digital publishing industry, with the expertise to create digital content for publishers across a vast range of subject matter. In addition to providing original digital content for third party publishers, we also republish civilization's greatest literary works, bringing them to new generations of readers via ebooks.

Sign up here to receive updates about free books as we publish them, and visit Our Kindle Author Page to browse today's free promotions and our most recently published Kindle titles.

Introduction

A picture of the Proton-K rocket

The Russian Space Program

Of all the goals the Bolshevik Revolution aimed to bring about, perhaps nowhere were Russian promises delivered on more than in the success of the Soviet Space program of the 1950s and 1960s. As a result of Russian innovation and technology, but also due to incredible drive to modernize and compete with the United States for world power, Russia was finally and triumphantly modernized in the eyes of her own people and the world. Neil deGrasse Tyson recognized the Soviet legacy in space in his *Space Chronicles*, citing the Soviets' "important measure[s] of space achievement: first spacewalk, longest spacewalk, first woman in space, first docking in space, first space station, longest time logged in space."[1]

In fact, the Soviet Union spent much of the 1950s leaving the United States in its dust (and rocket fuel). President Eisenhower and other Americans who could view Soviet rockets in the sky were justifiably worried that Soviet satellites in orbit could soon be spying on them, or, even worse, dropping nuclear bombs on them. Dovetailing off their success developing intercontinental ballistic missiles, the Soviets were the first to make enormous advances in actual space exploration, and on the night of October 4, 1957, the Soviets prepared to launch "Object D" atop one of its R-7 rockets. As the world's first ICBMs, R-7 rockets were built primarily to carry nuclear warheads, but "Object D" was a far different payload. "Object D" and the R-7 rocket launched from a hastily constructed launch pad, and within minutes it entered orbit. It took that object, now more famously known as Sputnik-1, about 90 minutes to complete its orbit around the Earth, speeding along at 18,000 miles per hour while transmitting a distinct beeping noise by radio.

Thanks to its transmission, and the bright mark it created in nighttime skies across the world, the world was already aware of the launch and orbit of Sputnik-1 before the Soviets formally announced the successful launch and orbit of their satellite. Naturally, the West wasn't thrilled to learn about the Soviets' launch of the first artificial object into Earth's orbit. Sputnik-1 could be measured in inches, but that large rocket it was attached to could wreak havoc if equipped with a nuclear warhead. Moreover, if Americans could see Sputnik-1, they were justifiably worried Sputnik-1 could see them.

In 1960, when Eisenhower's administration began planning and funding for the famous Apollo program that would land the first men on the Moon in 1969, the Soviet Union was already thinking further ahead, literally. In one of the worst kept secrets of the Space Race, the Soviet Union launched two probes, Korabl 4 and Korabl 5, toward Mars in October 1960.

Eventually, the Space Race produced some of the most iconic moments of the 20th century, including the landing of the first men on the Moon, and today, the race is widely viewed poignantly and fondly as a race to the Moon that culminated with Apollo 11 "winning" the race for the United States. In fact, it encompassed a much broader range of competition between the Soviet Union and the United States that affected everything from military technology to successfully launching satellites that could land on Mars or orbit other planets in the Solar System. Moreover, the notion that America "won" the Space Race at the end of the 1960s overlooks just how competitive the Space Race actually was in launching people into orbit, as well as the major contributions the Space Race influenced in leading to today's International Space Station and continued space exploration.

Soviet Russia's Space Program During the Space Race: The History and Legacy of the Competition that Pushed America to the Moon chronicles the history of Russia's space

---

[1] Neil deGrasse Tyson. Space Chronicles: Facing the Ultimate Frontier. (New York: W.W. Norton and Company, 2012). 6.

development and the competition it fostered. Along with pictures of important people, places, and events, you will learn about the Russian space program like never before, in no time at all.

Soviet Russia's Space Program During the Space Race: The History and Legacy of the Competition that Pushed America to the Moon

About Charles River Editors

Introduction

Chapter 1: Early Achievements

In 1721, Russia's Peter the Great began a 43 year reign over a Russia he was determined to bring into modern times. Embarking on a tour of modern capitals across Europe, he instituted a forced modernization of his own country that included building programs, increased taxation, and the construction of a modern capital and namesake, St. Petersburg. One of Peter's greatest goals was the modernization of the Russian army, both in its organization and in the technology of its weaponry. Advances in weapons technology, he promised, would provide Russia with the edge it needed to vault itself into modernity and catch up to the nations of Western Europe. Peter the Great even established Russia's first Academy of the Sciences in St. Petersburg, though the lack of Russian thinkers meant that, for the moment, the academy was staffed with scientists from Sweden and Germany.[2] Russia's future rulers, whether tsars or socialists, would continue to promise that technology and science would secure Russia's place amongst the nations.

---

[2] Brian Harvey and Olga Zakutnyaya. "Russian Space Probes: Scientific Discoveries and Future Missions." (Springer Science & Business Media, May 4, 2011), 1.

Peter the Great

Konstantin Tsiolkovsky, born in 1857, was the son of a Polish deportee to Siberia. A mathematician, inventor, and thinker, he is credited with the Tsiolkovsky formula which "established the relationships among rocket speed, the speed of the gas at exit, and the mass of the rocket and its propellant [and is] the basis of much of the spacecraft engineering."[3]

---

[3] "Konstantin E. Tsiolkovsky." NASA. September 22, 2010.

Tsiolkovsky

Looking for the earliest mention of manned space flight in Russian history, one finds a story recorded by Brian Harvey in his *Soviet and Russian Lunar Exploration*. He tells of a Soviet scientist, Mikhail Tikhonravov, who suggested a manned space flight in the pages of a children's magazine, which attracted the attention of both foreign governments and his own: "We do not have long to wait. We can assume that the bold dream of Tsiolkovsky will be realized within the next ten to fifteen years. All of you will become witnesses to this and some of you may even be participants in unprecedented journeys,"[4] he wrote to his audience of Soviet youth. Harvey writes of the early and little known collaboration of Tikhonravov and a then little known Russian military scientist by the name of Sergei Korolev, who would become the Soviets' chief designer and the mind behind much of the Soviet space achievement for almost two decades.

---

[4] Brian Harvey. *Russia in Space: The Failed Frontier?* (Chichester, UK: Praxis Publishing), 1.

Korolev

The Soviet space program started in earnest with the work of three scientists in the 1930s, but it would be a rough road to the earliest successes. Sergei Korolev, a Ukrainian technical student, along with fellow scientists, was recruited by the Soviet government in the early 1930s to incorporate their experiments with rockets, propelled by Glushko engines into the higher reaches, "where they could see the sky turn deep violet."[5] These early flights were conducted with balloons - either unmanned or manned, such as the flight of USSR I, and allowed Soviet scientists to collect information about air quality, the appearance of the sun, and the reaction of their craft to cosmic rays that proved important for later missions.[6] During Stalin's purge of the Soviet generals, many of these scientists became suspect, and some, including Korolev, spent time in prison camps. Korolev was a victim of one of hundreds of Stalinist purges when he and a list of 74 additional Russian scientists were accused and isolated for purging after the usual Stalinist show trial. The charges that led to Korolev's conviction consisted of utterly ludicrous "Crimes in the field of a new technology."[7]

Korolev was said to have shared the experience of his trial and conviction with two cosmonauts, Yuri Gagarin and Alexei Leonov, many years later. He told of being questioned by three Soviet officials after being arrested without warning at his home in 1938. His trial, according to Korolev, lasted only one minute, after he was required to read off a list of three specific charges. Korolev denied the charges.[8] Korolev, unlike many others, was not slated for

[5] Ibid., 3.
[6] Harvey and Zakutnyaya, 6.
[7] Matthew Brzezinski. *Red Moon Rising*. (New York: Henry Holt and Company, 2007), 33.

immediate execution, but was given a ten year sentence in a forced labor camp where he endured among other things, a broken jaw that never healed correctly. After serving only a few months of his sentence, the needs for the Russians to develop better weaponry for WWII meant that Korolev was released. He spent over six months attempting to return to Moscow in the icy, Russian winter and upon his return, he was allowed only to live in a dormitory with fellow scientists and weapons developers, not to return home to his wife and children.[9]

Gagarin

Though Korolev understood well that the rocket research he performed was targeted for pursuit of intercontinental ballistic missile launchers, he "always designed the rocket with a secondary purpose in mind: to open the door to space travel."[10] Khrushchev was leading the Soviets in an aggressive and public push for Intercontinental Ballistic Missile development. As tensions between the U.S. and the U.S.S.R continued to escalate, the countries were in competition in

[8] Alexei Leonov and David Scott. *Two Sides of the Moon: Our Story of the Cold War Space Race.* (New York: Thomas Dunne Books, 2006), 138.
[9] Ibid., 138-141.
[10] Harvey and Zakutnyaya, 6.

weapons development and in the race for world leadership. In *Space Travel: A History*, Wernher Von Braun argues that the United States' more sophisticated development of military weaponry was what actually caused the Soviets to appear to leap ahead with the eventual launch of Sputnik. While the U.S. concentrated on the development of smaller warheads that could be launched by ICBMs, the Soviets "went ahead and developed the massive rockets needed to carry its primitive bombs —the same vehicles that later gave it a significant advantage in space exploration."[11] The argument over whether or not the Soviets were actually ahead or only appeared ahead of the rest of the world in the 1950s and 1960s space program is one for historians today, but in the months leading to Sputnik's launch, the rivalry was anything but theoretical. In August of 1957, the Soviet's TASS news agency delivered this message about their military superiority and potential for dominance: "A few days ago a super long range, intercontinental multistage ballistic missile was launched...Covering an enormous distance in a short time, the missile hit the assigned region. The results obtained show that there is the possibility of launching missiles into any region of the terrestrial globe."[12]

---

[11] Wernher von Braun, Frederick I. Ordway III, and Dave Dooling. *Space Travel: A History*. (New York: Harper and Row, 1985), 164.
[12] Tyson, 123.

Von Braun

William Burrows, a professor of journalism and feature writer on space and aviation, explains Nikita Khrushchev's motives and his support for the burgeoning Soviet space program as political, and not merely strategic. As the Soviet Union continued to struggle from behind to catch her rivals in the west, and America's new president, John F. Kennedy, began calling for further exploration, "Khrushchev had become convinced that excelling in space (or seeming to) not only had immense propaganda values at home and abroad, but was relatively cheap for what it bought. And what it bought was the appearance of strength; a defensive mirage. Technology was the embodiment of socialism's triumph over nature and had long been the state religion. But its most important icon was no longer the tractor, the hydroelectric plant, or even the hydrogen bomb. It was the rocket."[13]

---

[13] William E. Burrows. *The New Ocean: The Story of the First Space Age*. (New York: Random House, 1998), 303.

Khrushchev

Soviet Premier Khrushchev's rocky rise to power had included a close call with an ouster in the summer of 1957. Khrushchev, it was felt by several members of the Presidium, had been rash in his commentary regarding the United States' ability to keep up with the Soviets in agricultural production: "We will bury you!," he had famously declared in reference to Soviet agricultural output goals. They mockingly accused him of having "become the expert on everything- from agriculture to science to culture."[14] He was, in fact, ousted as first secretary of the party, but in a precedent-setting turn of events, used his support amongst members of the central committee to overturn the vote of the Presidium.[15]

Khrushchev knew that to maintain power he would need the continued support of many on the Central Committee. This support could be maintained, he believed, with specific accomplishments in the fields of weapon's development and accomplishments in space. Khrushchev preferred the former, but competition with the United States in any form in those Cold War days was worthy enough of his attention and of funding and support.

Mathew Brzezinski records the story of Khrushchev's visit to Korolev's design laboratories in 1956. Here, Korolev revealed the potential of the rockets in development, as well as the missiles they would launch. Khrushchev stared at a classified map that revealed which countries rockets and missiles already developed and tested could strike. "How many warheads would be needed to destroy England? Have you calculated that?"[16] The answer came back with a claim and a confidence level that astonished Khrushchev: "Five would be enough to crush defenses and disrupt communications and transportation, not to mention the destruction of major cities."[17] Khrushchev was stunned and at first a bit skeptical. The V-2 rocket, developed at the end of WWII by German scientists and used at the end of the war, was Khrushchev's ideas of the ultimate deadly weapon. The fact that the Americans were attempting to develop technology with Wernher Von Braun, one of the V-2's creators, had long made the Soviets nervous. Now, an incredulous Khrushchev was told that the R-7 could go "four times faster and forty times further than the original V-2."[18] Trying to grasp its speed, Khrushchev tried to gain perspective, asking how long it would take the rocket to fly from Moscow to Kiev, a three hour flight for conventional planes. The answer: one minute.[19]

---

[14] Brzezinski, 110-1.
[15] Ibid., 112.
[16] Brzezinski, 37.
[17] Ibid.
[18] Ibid., 40.
[19] Ibid.

Chapter 2: Sputnik

A replica of Sputnik

Eventually, the successful launch of a Soviet satellite and the ensuing space race with the United States brought the rivalry between the United States and the Soviets to the attention of the world, but at first, the Soviet government seemed to merely tolerate what seemed like a "hobby" of the scientists working on launchers for ICBMs. Sergei Korolev, however, successfully convinced Khrushchev that the Soviets could launch a successful satellite, amounting to "single-handedly wav[ing] the opening flag in the space race."[20]

---

[20] John Mahoney. "Fifty Years Later, Looking Back at the Dawn of the Space Race". *Popular Science Magazine*, October 4, 2007.

It was during the 1956 meeting that Korolev made his pitch for what would become known as Sputnik. At the conclusion of Khrushchev's tour of the design laboratories, Korolev revealed his project, but the lack of understanding of what a satellite was and what its successful launch would represent on behalf of Khrushchev and other Soviet officials was clear to Korolev. He convinced Khrushchev to allow him to move ahead with Sputnik's development on two grounds: that an R-7 capable of launching a satellite was also capable of launching a warhead, and that the United States was in process of developing a satellite as well. Korolev persuaded the Soviet leader that Russia had a chance to beat them, meaning Khrushchev could get what he wanted in significant weapons development as well as have the chance to beat the Americans at something Korolev seemed to think was significant. His answer came back, "If the main task [weapons development] doesn't suffer, do it."[21]

After several experimental rockets, Korolev and others became convinced they could create a rocket launcher powerful enough to put a satellite into orbit. The R-7 that had been introduced to Khrushchev during the design bureau visit represented, as Korolev put it, not the past and present of Soviet rocketry but the future.[22] In hindsight, according to Brzezinski at least, Korolev had overpromised in his attempt to convince Khrushchev to allow development of the satellite project to move forward, because the R-7 rocket that had been so proudly revealed as the "future" of Soviet military dominance was "an illusion, little more than a ten-story-tall modeler's toy. The real prototype was nowhere near ready."[23]

Nonetheless, Soviet engineers and designers continued their labor, readying several satellite candidates at one time. As time for the launch drew closer, it was determined that the more complicated satellite that some had hoped would be ready to launch needed to be put on hold. The "ton-and-a-half cone studded with antennas"[24] would be put on hold (and later launched as Sputnik 3). In the meantime, the "polished ball" that author William E. Burrows calls "Korolev's last choice" would be readied for launch.

Sputnik was launched into space just before midnight on October 4, 1957, and the R-7 rocket launcher was successful in putting the "preliminary satellite"[25] into orbit. Korolev took a moment to speak with his fellow scientists, saying, "Today, the dreams of the best sons of mankind have come true. The assault on space has begun."[26] The news was greeted by the world with shock and surprise; there had been consistent rumors of Soviet attempts to ready for a launch into space, but most Americans assumed they were still a long ways off from success. The Soviets were "gently" criticized by members of the scientific community of five nations that had gathered in Washington D.C. in 1957, to which the Soviets responded by "saying they

[21] Brzezinski, 44.
[22] Brzezinski, 39.
[23] Ibid., 64-5.
[24] William E. Burrows. *This New Ocean: The Story of the First Space Age.* (New York: Random House, 1998).3.
[25] Ibid., 4.
[26] Ibid., 39.

considered it unseemly to 'boast' about experiments until they were complete. 'We will not cackle until we have laid our egg.'" In the midst of the gathering of some of the world's most formidable scientists, the news arrived that a Russian satellite was circling ahead. The majority of the scientists present seemed surprised but pleased at the news, and congratulations were given to the Soviets, who were suddenly the celebrities of the event. [27]

The importance of Sputnik in both Soviet history and the history of space exploration in general cannot be overstated. Not only did Sputnik encourage Soviet pride in having beaten the Americans to an important milestone, it "inaugurated the first triumphant decade of Soviet space exploration, as one after another, Soviet space exploits inscribed a new glorious cosmic future into the fabric of a popular imagination. A row of hero cosmonauts circle the earth in increasingly ambitious ventures in their Vostok and Voskhod spaceships."[28]

The satellite itself, weighing 184 pounds, was surprisingly simple.[29] Korolev led the team of scientists and engineers to create Sputnik, "a sphere of aluminum alloys with four spring loaded whip antennas and two battery-powered radio transmitters" …it was fitted "within a pointed metal nose cone."[30] In order to ensure the satellite was constructed to his specifications, Korolev not only participated in but directly supervised construction and launch, living on site "halfway between the rocket assembly building and the R-7 launchpad."[31]

Pravda reported on October 5th, "The successful launching of the first man-made earth satellite makes an important contribution to the treasure-house of world science and culture…Artificial earth satellites will pave the way for interplanetary travel and apparently our contemporaries will witness how the freed and conscientious labor of the people of the new socialist society makes the most daring dreams of mankind a reality."[32]

Sputnik itself was derided by Eisenhower as nothing more than "one small ball in the air,"[33] but impressively, the Soviets had completed construction of the satellite in three months once Khrushchev had given the green light to the project. The ball itself was made of aluminum, polished and surrounding a battery pack that emitted a distinctive beep that would allow both U.S. and Soviet scientists to confirm its orbit.[34] It would orbit the earth at a speed of over 18,000 miles per hour, which meant one elliptical revolution took about 96 minutes.[35]

---

[27] Dickson, 12-13.
[28] James T. Andrews and Asif A. Siddiqi, Ed. *Into the Cosmos: Space Exploration and Soviet Culture*. (Pittsburgh: University of Pittsburgh Press, 2011), 5.
[29] John Mahoney.
[30] Alan Shephard and Deke Slayton. "The Beginning". *Moon Shot: The Inside Story of America's Race to the Moon*. (Atlanta: Turner Publishing Inc., 1994), 37.
[31] Ibid., 37.
[32] Tyson, 121.
[33] Robert A. Divine. *The Sputnik Challenge*. (Oxford University Press, 1993), 7.
[34] Ibid., xiv.
[35] Paul Dickson. *Sputnik: The Shock of a Century*. (Bloomsbury Publishing, 2009), 9.

Historians agree that the American response to the Soviet's initial space success in Sputnik was generally dismay, and in some circles, shock. Americans were able not only to hear Sputnik's beeps over the radio but see the satellite in the night sky over the United States. A photograph of two young American boys, backs to the camera, looking up at the shining Russian satellite from behind a railing is the opening image to Paul Dickson's *Sputnik: The Shock of the Century*.[36] Edwin Marcus's cartoon shows a rudely awakened Uncle Sam in his nightshirt, sitting up in a bed called "complacency" with Sputnik beeping loudly from the sky outside his bedroom window. The caption below asks the simple but significant question, "Awake at Last?"[37]

The country reacted with fear, partly led by those who appeared to have reason to know. Edward Teller, inventor of the hydrogen bomb, said that the launch of Sputnik meant that the U.S. "had lost a battle more important and greater than Pearl Harbor."[38] Though later historians would come to discount the military significance of Sputnik (since the R-7 launcher used to put Sputnik into orbit was not capable of successfully launching ICBMs), one could safely say that "there was a sudden crisis of confidence in American technology, values, politics, and the military."[39]

---

[36] Ibid.
[37] Edwin Marcus. "Awake At Last?" Library of Congress Prints and Photographs Division. Washington, D.C. 1957.
[38] Dickson, 4.
[39] Ibid.

Teller

Khrushchev took full advantage of the surprise, pointing out, "People of the whole world are pointing to the satellite. They are saying that the U.S. has been beaten."[40] Should the United States have been as surprised as with the public claims that the Soviets had been making? Perhaps not, but "Americans, who had become accustomed to laughing at Russia's technological efforts…suddenly [found] themselves in the uncomfortable position of second place in a two-horse race."[41] The suspicion and fear would continue with each Soviet triumph.

---

[40] Shephard and Slayton, 42.

Though there is little debate about the immediate American response to Sputnik's launch, much has been written about Sputnik's actual significance and of the success of the Russian space program over time. Many Americans viewed Sputnik as a sign that the United States had fallen behind militarily, while others argued that the country had fallen behind in the larger context of scientific inquiry. Some historians, however, have come to the conclusion that while the launch of Sputnik took the American science community by surprise, it did not mean that the Soviets had achieved military superiority of any kind. In fact, author Harry Hopkinson claims Sputnik functioned as less of an example of Soviet military strength and more as a strategic bluff on the part of Khrushchev, a scare tactic that the Soviet leader employed to help establish the United States' acceptance of a "peaceful coexistence" with a Soviet Union that was actually far weaker than it was purported to be.[42]

In their book *Moon Shot: The Inside Story of America's Race to the Moon,* Alan Shepard and Deke Slayton argue that the Eisenhower administration had ignored warnings and signs that the Soviets would reach space before the United States. Their claim includes charges that Wernher von Braun, a German scientist recruited by the American military after the defeat of the Nazis, asked for permission to launch a project of his own design, a satellite known as Missile 29. If so, the reasons for such a refusal are still widely debated. It's possible Eisenhower wanted an American and not a German scientist to get credit for the initial launch, and some think the administration demanded that the first American satellite be disassociated with military efforts and seen as purely scientific. Whatever the case, Eisenhower ordered Braun's project be placed in storage, ensuring the Russians had "an open door and a free ride to lead the world into tomorrow."[43]

Debates over geopolitical context aside, the launch of Sputnik I is largely hailed as the opening moment of the true "Space Race" not only because of the fame and fear inspired by the launch but also because its purpose was not entirely one of military value. While the Sputnik satellite indicated the Soviets had significant military advantages in potentially weaponizing space, Sputnik's value was not exclusively military. Had something like Sputnik-1 been America's goal in 1957, it very likely could have accomplished this important first. Von Braun had successfully designed the Jupiter-C rocket by 1956, which could have allowed the United States to launch a satellite like Sputnik-1 into space a year before the Soviets did, but at the time, however, the technology was being designed for use as missiles. In response to Sputnik-1, Eisenhower quickly ordered an attempt to put a satellite in orbit. Thus, a Space Race of a more civilian nature was launched alongside Sputnik. The two superpowers would now compete to inspire the world with their ingenuity.

---

[41] Von Braun, Ordway III, and Dooling. 171.
[42] Harry Hopkinson. *Bluff of the Century: Sputnik and the Cold War.*
[43] Shephard and Slayton, 31-36.

Chapter 3: Sputnik 2 and Sputnik 3

It was important to Khrushchev that the path for manned flight was laid - and Laika the dog would seem to do just that - while the Americans had yet to successfully put a satellite into orbit.[44] Khrushchev's timeline for the second satellite demanded that Korolev produce it in time for the anniversary of the Russian Revolution in November.[45] This, along with Khrushchev's realization that the capitalist world had been quite shaken by the announcement of the successful Soviet satellite, meant the need for a repeat performance to capitalize on world reaction and international prowess escalated.[46] As a result, Laika would catch a ride to space board Sputnik 2.

Laika, a female Samoyed nicknamed "The Barker,"[47] was selected for the journey to space and provided with the necessities to support life for one week. Telemetry was provided in order to communicate important information about Laika's condition throughout the first week of orbit. Vitals such as the dog's temperature, blood pressure, and breathing rate were gathered through instruments that had been specifically made for Laika (some surgically installed) and had been part of her training for the past several months. The plan was for Laika to be fed poison or to run out of oxygen after the battery power failed, but according to Soviet records revealed years after the collapse of communism, Laika died within a few hours of being in orbit due to freezing conditions in the satellite. Some have claimed that the death happened even before that time, since torn insulation may have allowed the temperatures on board the satellite to grow higher than 100 degrees.[48]

The Soviet people had a chance to hear Laika by radio when she was introduced to the public in anticipation of the launch in November.[49] Some authors have remarked on the negative response of some of the Soviet people (as well as the rarity of public criticism of government decisions) regarding Laika's journey to space and inevitable death. One of Laika's trainers, the Russian scientist Oleg Gazenko, remarked as late as 1998, "The more time passes, the more I'm sorry about it. We did not learn enough from the mission to justify the death of the dog."[50]

---

[44] Jamie Doran and Piers Bizony. *Starman: The Truth Behind the Legend of Yuri Gagarin.* (New York: Walker Publishing Company. 2011), 51.

[45] Lance K. Erickson. *Space Flight: History, Technology, and Operations.* (Roman and Littlefield, 2010). 580.

[46] Ibid.

[47] Ibid., 582.

[48] Colin Burgess and Chris Dubbs. *Animals in Space: From Research Rockets to the Space Shuttle.* (Springer Science and Business Media, 2007), 164.

[49] Burgess and Dubbs, 156-158.

[50] Ibid., 165.

Laika

As for Sputnik 2 itself, the satellite was launched only three weeks after[51] the Soviet's initial victory with the satellite. Compared to the 184 pound Sputnik, Sputnik 2 weighed 1,120 pounds.[52] William Burrows notes Sputnik 2's importance in the space race, citing multiple reasons. First, the successful launch solidified the Soviet achievement for anyone who had doubted the veracity of the Sputnik launch and orbit. Sputnik 2's weight of over 1000 pounds was also confirmation of Soviet ICBM capability. Lastly, the sophistication of Sputnik 2 meant that the Russians had every intention of using their space program to gain further knowledge about the world and, eventually, to send a human to gather it.[53]

---

[51] Ibid., 4.
[52] Ibid., 44.
[53] Burrows, 198-9.

A model of Sputnik 2

Sputnik 3 began its orbit May 15, 1958. Its main purpose was to measure, taking readings of the earth's upper atmosphere and radiation.[54] The launch of the 5000 pound satellite that was Korolev's first choice less than a year before Sputnik 1 was substituted shows the advances of both Soviet competence and confidence in a short period. Sputnik 3's launch also highlighted the sway that Korolev held over Khrushchev, whose military opposed another Sputnik launch and were openly accusing Korolev of being "too wrapped up in space."[55] Political infighting, competing loyalties, and the rivalry between the military, the Soviet space program, and those vying for power and leadership meant that several programs would compete for attention and funding. While the goal of manned space flight was clearly on the agenda, unmanned flights that would push the envelope and keep the Soviets in the record books were also worthy of attention.

---

[54] Von Braun, Ordway III, and Dooling, 171.
[55] Brzezinski, 246.

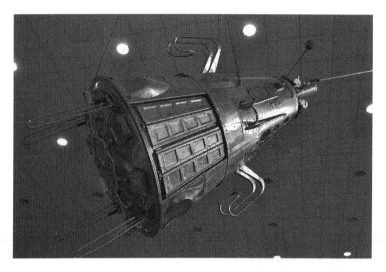

Sputnik 3

Chapter 4: The Luna Program

Luna I was intended to be an impactor. The ball, with some significant resemblance to Sputnik, was to impact the moon and intended to give guidance to the Soviets about potential future missions there. In order to escape the orbital path it was otherwise destined for, Luna I was equipped with a rocket system designed to be put into use well into the launch. This rocket would put Luna in the path of the moon and allow the moon's gravitational pull to capture the probe. Instead, an error by ground control crews meant that Luna would miss the moon by more than 5,000 kilometers and become an orbiting "artificial planet" instead, the first craft to escape geocentric orbit. Luna I also released a bright orange colored gas that allowed scientists to track its path visually.

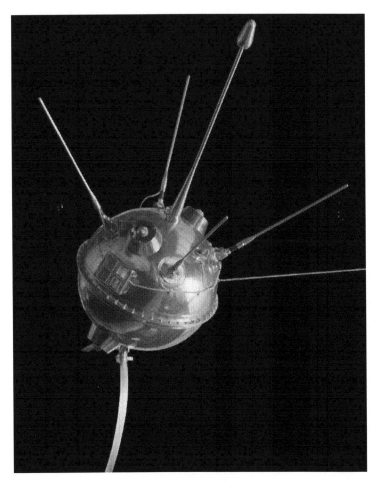

A replica of Luna I

In September of 1959, Luna 2 was launched, another attempt to reach the moon with an impactor, or a device that would hit the moon and was not intended to return or land without damage. Luna 2 hit the desired target with precision, indicating to the world not only the Soviets' ability to land a "man-made object on a heavenly body" but also a rapidly developing accuracy.[56]

---

[56] De Groot, 98.

Luna 2

Luna 3 made a successful journey to photograph the far side of the moon on October 4, 1959. This was another important accomplishment for the Soviets, as Luna 3 "had to fly between the Sun and the Moon, stop its rotation, point and shoot its two cameras for forty minutes while the attitude control system kept it steady and then head back to earth so the imagery could be scanned electronically and transmitted to ground stations by television as the spacecraft swung by from 25,000 miles out."[57] Luna 3's 27 photographs also "had a predictable effect upon American self-confidence, demonstrating once again that Korolev had a keen sense of how to use his rockets to dent the American ego."[58]

---

[57] Burrows, 363.
[58] De Groot, 98.

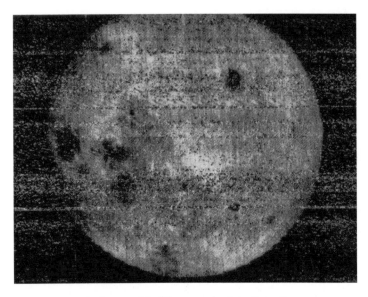

An image of the Moon sent back by Luna 3

With the Luna missions, the Soviets tried to further their goal of being first to the moon while avoiding the immediate cost and awaiting the technological breakthroughs required for a manned landing. Luna 9 made a successful soft landing in February of 1967, but that success followed "at least five previous attempts" by the Soviets.[59] By the time Luna 15 attempted a moon landing to pick up soil samples in July of 1969, in the midst of the American moon landing, it was official: the Soviets had lost the race to put a man on the moon. Luna 15 crashed along with the Soviet hopes to claim another space first.[60] Soviet cosmonaut Alexei Leonov described his own reaction, as well as the reaction of the Soviet scientific community, to the news that the Americans had landed on the moon: "If it couldn't be me, let it be this crew, I thought, with what we in Russia call 'white envy' envy mixed with admiration…Even in the military center where I stood, where military men were observing the achievements of our rival superpower, there was loud applause."[61]

---

[59] Burrows, 394.
[60] De Groot, 236.
[61] De Groot, 238.

Leonov (left)

Luna missions also had the goal of reaching Mars and Venus first, but there were several failures along the way (in fact an over 50% failure rate, though lower than the American rate).[62] William Burrows suggests a link between manned and unmanned Luna missions in that successful unmanned missions were always indications to the Americans that a manned flight with similar goals was soon to follow.[63] Soviet cosmonauts of the future would become more and

---

[62] Burrows, 345.

more frustrated with automata, believing that the human role was being replaced by less expensive and less risky unmanned exploration.

The Luna missions continued, in competition with other Soviet efforts (including manned missions), throughout the 1960s and '70s. Though the Soviets had later success, such as Luna 16 and 17's soft landings and data and photography collection, "they would in effect amount to toys that crawled in the shadow of the astronauts."[64]

The last of the Luna missions took place in 1976 when Luna 24 made a successful soft landing on the moon and collected a soil sample after drilling approximately two meters into the moon's surface. At the time, the Russian claim to have found water on the moon was ignored by many Western scientists who believed that the soil samples collected by the Apollo missions had proven that there was no water on the moon. Later astrophysicists, such as Arlin Crotts, now credit the Soviet Luna 24 mission as properly gathering a sample with reliable measurements.[65]

Chapter 5: The Vostok Missions

Three years after Sputnik 2 had taken Laika into orbit, the Soviets were ready again to use canines in space, and this time with a provision for the animals to return safely to earth. Obviously, the recovery of an animal after space flight was an important hurdle that had to be cleared before a manned flight could be considered. Thus, two dogs selected from the space program's trained canine group were to take part in the first Vostok mission: Belka and Strelka.[66] Like Laika, the new canine cosmonauts would be launched from the Baikonur facility.

Burgess and Dubbs outline several concerns regarding the Vostok program. First was the concern that an adequate heat shield could be developed to protect life upon re-entry into the earth's atmosphere. Second, it was important to determine whether sufficient systems for supporting life could be put in place. Lastly, the Soviets wanted to see if the effects on the space traveler, whether human or canine could be measured, predicted, and dealt with. Naturally, the Soviets, criticized both at home and abroad for the death of Laika in Sputnik 2, also wanted to ensure the safe return of Belka and Strelka for moral reasons as well.[67]

Despite problems that were not anticipated during flight, Belka and Strelka returned to Earth after 25 hours and made it through re-entry alive and well. In the aftermath, Belka and Strelka became Soviet celebrities, pictured on advertisements, postcards, and sought out for photo-ops with Soviet politicians.[68] One of Strelka's puppies was later given as a gift to Jacqueline Kennedy, though Burgess and Dubbs report that the dog had to undergo multiple tests to ensure

[63] Ibid., 346.
[64] Ibid., 428.
[65] "Soviet Moon Lander Discovered Water on the Moon in 1976." *MIT Technology Review*. May 30, 2012.
[66] Burgess and Dubbs, 202-203.
[67] Oliver Wainwright. "The Dogs that Conquered Space." The Guardian. September 2, 2014.
[68] Ibid.

it was not outfitted with any type of spying device.[69]

The two space dogs

Training for Soviet cosmonauts who would soon enter space for the first time took place in Star City, a highly secret training ground in Kazakhstan. The Cosmonaut Training Center's construction was ordered by the Soviet Ministry of Defense in January of 1960.[70] Baikonur's location in Kazakhstan was not only a practical choice but a philosophical one that emerged from the Soviet attitude toward its space program and its designers and cosmonauts, according to the authors of *Epic Rivalry: The Inside Story of the Soviet and American Space Race.* The Soviets, in contrast to the Americans, built "a sealed-off world, always detached and inaccessible, a military precinct carefully hidden from public scrutiny."[71] The Kazakh location provided practical advantages as well: enough room for easy recovery of re-entry vehicles, the space needed for the number of launch pads, dual radio stations, and other ground support for launches, and the location nearer to the earth's equator.[72]

A look at the website of Gagarin Cosmonaut Training Center at Star City, as it is known today, is a reminder of the earliest decisions in Russian space history. Korolev is quoted as recommending air force pilots as future cosmonauts: [Air force pilots] "are trained better than anyone else, especially fighter pilots. A jet fighter pilot is a required universal person. He flies a single-seat, high-speed jet in the stratosphere. He is a pilot, an air navigator, an operator and a

---

[69] Burgess and Dubbs, 207.

[70] Michael Cassutt. "Star City at 50". *Air and Space Magazine*. Smithsonian. March 2011.

[71] Von Hardesty, and Gene Eisman. Epic Rivalry: The inside Story of the Soviet and American Space Race. (Washington, D.C.: National Geographic, 2007), 138.

[72] Ibid., 143.

flight engineer at the same time..."[73]

Despite the fact that the Soviet cosmonauts, as well as others from around the world in later years, have trained at Star City for over 50 years, much about the place has remained secret. The only published and dedicated work on Star City to date is by a Dutch author and researcher, Bert Vis, who was allowed multiple visits after 1991.[74]

The Soviet training dynamic made Star City unique from the beginning. It was decided that the style would be like that of a campus, an isolated place where cosmonauts would not only train, but live. A wooded area 25 miles north of the nearest city was selected, one that allowed it to remain relatively hidden away but to maintain access to the Soviet air base nearby.[75] Vis's book contrasts the American approach to training flight crews to the Soviet approach. While the Americans trained a crew for each mission, as well as potential individuals to serve as replacements if necessary, crews at Star City were trained as wholes, usually in groups of two or three. If a flight crew member needed to be replaced, it was likely that the other members of the crew would be replaced as well.[76] Final selections for a flight were made known very close to the actual launch of the mission and kept secret, even from family members. For example, Yuri Gagarin's relatives only found out about his successful launch from news announcements.

Though eventually Star City would grow large enough to encompass almost all areas of training, it at first served an administrative role and as the center of physical training for the cosmonauts. Technological training for missions, as well as simulation took place elsewhere, partly because of the limited facility (at its opening, Star City had only one two-story building) and partly because of infighting between those who built the spacecrafts and the trainers of the cosmonauts themselves.[77]

In time, the facility would grow to include multiple buildings, a gymnasium, dormitories, flight simulators, and a pool over the next 5-7 years, but funds and permissions were sometimes hard to come by and definitely unpredictable. The Soviet government allocated funds as they saw fit, at times heeding the call of the directors of Star City, and at times ignoring them. While the facility might have money dedicated to major projects, it seems at times the most practical needs went unmet. Vis relates a story from the diary of Kamamin, Star City's early director, about attempts to obtain transportation for cosmonauts to facilities in Crimea and Baikonur. Despite some state-of-the-art technology, the provisions for living conditions and the convenience of the cosmonauts were not foremost concerns, it seems. Kamamin complains that his cosmonauts were, at times, reduced to hitchhiking in order to get to the training facilities for water recovery or mission

[73] YU.A. Gagarin Research and Test Cosmonaut Training Center. "GCTC History". Russian Federal Space Agency.
[74] Ibid.
[75] Rex Hall, Shayler David, and Bert Vis. *Russian Cosmonauts: Inside the Yuri Gagarin Training Center*. (Springer Science & Business Media, Oct 5, 2007), 1.
[76] Hall, David, and Vis, xxxiii.
[77] Ibid.

control, creating potential safety issues.

Despite the difficulties faced by the Russian cosmonauts, the Soviets would beat their rival to the next space feat: manned space flight. This can be credited to the way the Soviet program developed, with concentration on ballistic missiles, then sounding rockets (designed to gather information from the upper atmosphere or just into space) and finally to spacecraft that could be launched by carrier vehicles.[78]

Yuri Gagarin entered Vostock I on April 12, 1961, chosen out of 20 cosmonauts in his training program at Baikonur for the first manned space mission. Gagarin was unknown to the outside world, though his name and desire for information about his background would increase greatly upon his return from space. As Hall, David, and Vis explain in *Russia's Cosmonauts*, the Russian tradition of cosmonaut training focuses on anonymity until a mission has been launched. This way, for those who trained as cosmonauts but were never selected for space flight, their names remain unknown to the rest of the world and the Russian scientific community.[79]

Rodgers speculates that Khrushchev made the final decision for Gagarin because of their similar peasant backgrounds, though his main competitor, Gherman Titov, was later to say that the right choice had been made since Gagarin was a better public relations choice.[80] Indeed, authors Jamie Doran and Piers Bizony argue that Gagarin is the only example of a Soviet hero, since "to be a hero under communism is an anomaly, for no individual could be greater than the collective whole."[81]

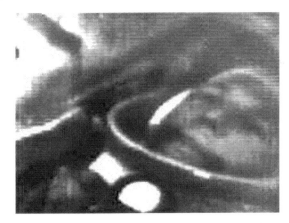

[78] Von Braun, Ordway III, and Dooling, 199.
[79] Hall, David, and Vis.
[80] Paul Rodgers. "Yuri Gagarin: The Man Who Fell to Earth." *The Independent*. April 3, 2011.
[81] Doran and Bizony, 1.

Gagarin in the space capsule

Though it is easy to see (and common for Americans to believe) that early space cosmonauts or astronauts were pioneers deserving of recognition and respect, when one realizes the level of unknown that these men and women faced, their status as heroes becomes even more clear. When Gagarin took flight in Vostok I, he had only experienced weightlessness for 2 to 3 seconds, courtesy of a free-falling elevator in a tall building in Moscow. The elevator car's descent would be stopped by blowers at the bottom of the 28 story shaft, allowing cosmonauts to experience only a glimpse of a world without gravity.[82] In fact, Doran and Bizony state that the Soviets had no particular confidence that a man could survive a 24-hour period without gravity, so new was the concept. The American space program used stripped cargo planes flown in "parabolic arcs" that would allow up to two minutes of gravity-free flight for astronauts in training.[83]

No matter what kind of preparations were taken, space flight was unpredictable, and the risks were many. Additionally, one of the largest areas of concern for the Soviets was the public relations coup, and not primarily safety of the cosmonauts. The space program and government prepared three envelopes to be released to the press after the launch of Vostok I: one in case of complete success, in which Gagarin's victory would be broadcast to the world; one in case the capsule or the parachuting Gagarin descended onto foreign territory; and one in case of disaster, such as an explosion or the capsule being lost in space and unable to return to Earth, dooming Gagarin to death from thirst, starvation, or lack of oxygen, whichever came first.[84]

---

[82] Ibid., 65.
[83] Ibid., 66.
[84] Ibid. 66-68.

A model of Vostok 1

Vostok 1 weighed over 5 tons, and the spacecraft itself was called Swallow. Before the launch, Gagarin was assisted into his orange cosmonaut suit and approached the elevator before speaking to those who were invited to the observation: "At this instant, the whole of my life seems to be condensed into one wonderful moment. Everything that I have experienced, everything that I have done hitherto, was experienced and done for the sake of this moment...Of course, I'm happy. In all times and epochs the greatest happiness for man has been to take part in new discoveries. To be first to enter the cosmos, to engage, single-handed, in an unprecedented duel with nature….could one dream of anything more!"[85]

Gagarin left earth at 9:07 a.m. Moscow time,[86] and during his 89 minute orbit, he experienced weightlessness: "Up and down no longer existed. He was suspended in physical limbo, kept from floating about loosely only by the harness strapping him to his contoured couch. About him the magic of weightlessness appeared in the form of papers, a pencil, his notebook, and other objects drifting, responding to the gentle tugs of air from his life-support system fans."[87]

---

[85] Peter Bond. *Heroes in Space: From Gagarin to Challenger.* (Basil Blackwell Inc., 1987), 14.
[86] Ibid., 94.
[87] Ibid., 95.

The flight lasted just a few hours, with Gagarin returning to Earth by braking at the edge of the atmosphere, ejecting from the capsule at a planned point, and then parachuting to the ground. The actions of ejection and parachuting came close to costing the Russians their place in history, as one of the rules in place for space flight records required that the vessel that was launched returned to Earth still manned. In the case of both Vostok 1 and 2, the cosmonauts ejected, as planned, from the capsule.

Announcements issued from the Soviet government were hazy about the connection between cosmonaut and vessel, committing only to reports that both cosmonaut and vehicle touched down "somewhere near" a designated field. This controversy was settled later when it was determined that the manned orbit of space, and not the landing, was what mattered for scientific records.

After the Soviets beat the United States to the first successful manned space mission, *Life Magazine* featured Yuri Gagarin greeting Khrushchev on its April 1961 cover, with the accompanying article's introduction including these lines of admission: "For men everywhere, this astounding exploit should have been a matter of pure exaltation. It was a victory for a long scientific effort in rocketry everywhere and the result of extraordinary preparations in Russia. The mysteries of outer space for the first time seemed to lie within the measure of human instruments. But even as Earth's gravity reasserted its pull upon the returning capsule, the agonizing ears and suspicions of the cold war moved in to tarnish Gagarin's courageous act. Nikita Khrushchev openly brandished at the West his new sign of Soviet power."[88]

The same article featured quotes from a section entitled "Some Reactions Overseas", a follow-up to its words on the reactions from Washington, from Kennedy to key senators and frustrated NASA scientists quoted anonymously. The quotes featured seem to promote the narrative of U.S. humiliation in front of a watching world: A German secretary realizes "Soviet boasts of ultimate superiority may not be groundless after all," while an African student in Paris remarks, "The Americans talked a lot. Russia kept silent until success came. The results speak for themselves."[89] It seemed in the immediate wake of Soviet news that any U.S. answers would be inadequate. Referencing the promised Mercury launch, *Life* declared, "Now, even if everything goes off on schedule and an Astronaut is launched late this month or early next, the achievement will seem pallid."[90]

While that didn't end up being true, the name Yuri Gagarin has become inseparable from Russian space history. A popular story recalls Gagarin's return to Earth from his trip in space in 1961. As two women, a mother and daughter, worked in a potato field, they were approached by a man in an orange space suit and white helmet.[91] He acknowledged that he had indeed come from space. As Paul Rodgers writes in *The Independent*, the legend of "a Soviet hero being

[88] "Soviet Traveler Returns From Out of This World". *Life Magazine*. (Vol. 50, No. 16. April 21, 1961).
[89] "Some Reactions Overseas". *Life Magazine*. (Vol. 50, No. 16. April 21, 1961), 27.
[90] Ibid.
[91] Paul Rodgers. Yuri Gagarin: The Man Who Fell to Earth. *The Independent*. April 3, 2011.

welcomed home by his fellow peasants, a wise mother and a child of the future"[92] fit the government's purposes perfectly, but was also likely "true in essence." Calling him "a poster boy for the Soviet space programme,"[93] Rodgers goes on to recount Gagarin's youth, growing up under collectivization and eventually being sent to technical school, where he experienced his first flight.

Gagarin, standing at only 5'2" (which was considered a positive in the days of early space flight), married only a few weeks after the launch of Sputnik and eventually was invited to take part in the cosmonaut training programs that resulted from the excitement for manned space travel.[94] *Life Magazine* reported that he had only recently become a member of the Communist Party (unlike the soon-to-be renowned Valentina Tereshkova), though he was quickly proclaimed a Soviet Hero, given military honors, and celebrated his triumph in Red Square at Lenin's sacred grave[95] saying to the crowds, "One can say with assurance that in Soviet spacecraft we will fly even over more distant routes. I am boundlessly happy that my beloved homeland was the first to accomplish this flight, was the first to reach outer space."[96]

As fate would have it, Gagarin never made another space flight, which would prove especially important in light of the controversy over Soyuz I, a capsule that some see as having been doomed to failure and one that Gagarin was supposed to man. Gagarin never repeated his space mission, but he remained involved with the program until his premature death in 1968 as a result of a crash of his MiG-15 test plane.

Many years of controversy and conspiracy have followed Gagarin's death, but a 2010 article in *The Telegraph* reported the claims of a Soviet investigator who had been studying Gagarin's crash for over seven years. The findings of the Russian study indicated that Gagarin's sudden and dramatic descent into a forest was likely a result of an overreaction - pilot error on the part of Gagarin when he realized that a vent on the MiG-15 had been left open. As the plane descended at rapid speed, it is now the conclusion of Russian investigative teams that Gagarin and his trainer blacked out and were unconscious at the time of the crash.[97] Gagarin's ashes were buried in the wall of the Kremlin, giving him a place of continued honor amongst other Soviet heroes.[98]

Subsequent Vostok missions followed closely on top of one another, largely for political reasons. Khrushchev desired an atmosphere of continual Soviet success and one that would put continual pressure on the Americans, as well as encourage the satellite countries to stay in line. Soviet scientists and engineers were by now used to launch times and priorities being set by anniversaries and the suspected progress of the U.S., not by particular readiness. Part of the

[92] Ibid.
[93] Ibid.
[94] Ibid.
[95] "Some Reactions Overseas".
[96] Bond, 17.
[97] Andrew Osborn. Yuri Gagarin Death Mystery Solved after Forty Years. *The Telegraph*. 8 January, 2010.
[98] Bond, 17.

timing for the landing of Vostok 2 was designed with the construction of the Berlin Wall in mind, a show of irresistible Soviet power and strength. Though the next two Vostok missions were similar in scope and length (a four day and three day mission), they gave off the deliberate illusion that the Soviets were accomplishing a "space rendezvous," an event in which two manned space flights made contact with one another. This was an exaggeration at best, but one the Soviets allowed to be assumed by observers who noted the parallel times of the flights: "With all the secrecy we had in those days, we didn't tell the whole truth…as they say, a sleight of hand isn't exactly a fraud. It was more like our competitors [in the east] deceived themselves all on their own. Of course, we didn't want to shatter their illusions."[99]

Cosmonaut Gherman Titov, who had been the backup cosmonaut for Vostok 1, was in orbit for 25 hours at only 25 years of age, making him the youngest person in space to this day.[100] Though his mission was later overshadowed by the many Vostoks and other missions to come, Titov understood the importance of flights that were not necessarily firsts but simply furthered the overall goal of space flight: "Now we must accumulate experience in construction of space technology, elaborate the methodology of training man to live on board spacecraft. I won't conceal that the Soviet space programme envisaged follow-up space flights. The Vostok 2 was ready to go. We awaited the opinions of medical specialists and biologists who analyzed the results of the first manned flight. We wanted to know, in particular, what impact space factors had on man's organism. Opinions on this differed. By no means everyone agreed, and certainly not at once, to the proposal of a 24 hour flight. It was suggested that we should limit ourselves to three or four, a maximum of six orbits. But why should we mark time?"[101]

---

[99] Ibid., 149.
[100] Ibid., 18.
[101] Ibid.

Titov

Titov, indeed, suffered from some space sickness during the flight, but he managed to carry out the experiments and communication as planned. He also slept in space, commenting, "I slept the sleep of the just and spent 35 minutes longer than envisaged by the programme. My sleep was good, without dreams. In contrast to earth conditions, I didn't feel the necessity of turning side to side."[102] However, Titov struggled with some aspects of recovery, particularly balance issues, causing some concern about man's ability to adjust to longer periods without gravity. Bond

---

[102] Ibid., 19.

speculates that this "may be why there were no more manned space flights for a year."[103]

Vostok 3 and 4 added to the manned Soviet space flight time, but they also had the distinction of being in orbit at the same time. Though the original intent had been for the flights to "rendezvous" to a limited extent, the orbital patterns were a bit off and they never came closer than 5 kilometers. It is important to note the accomplishments of the two missions, however, which not only continued to shock the world but also "demonstrate the Soviet capability to track an orbiting spacecraft accurately, to launch a craft into a pre-determined orbit accurately, and to control simultaneously two craft in orbit."[104]

Vostok 5 was launched June 14, 1963 with cosmonaut Valery Bykovsky aboard, answering to the call-sign Hawk,[105] and Vostok 6 was the latest Soviet accomplishment that appeared (on the surface, at least) to prove that the Soviets were ahead in the race to space milestones. Bykovsky orbited the planet for over 119 hours and safely returned to Earth in the same manner as previous Vostok missions by ejecting and parachuting to earth after re-entry. The Americans, in contrast, had just completed their longest manned-vehicle orbit with the Mercury mission in May of 1963, lasting only 34 hours.[106]

Bykovsky (left)

[103] Ibid.
[104] Ibid. 21.
[105] Shephard and Slayton, 166.
[106] Ibid.

Though Bykovsky's mission had set a new record for manned space flight, only two days into his mission, a new groundbreaking development was waiting on the launch pad in Baikonur. Valentina Tereshkova, the first woman in space, entered orbit, along with Bykovsky, on June 16, 1963 on Vostok 6. She had been selected from a team of five female cosmonauts chosen for training. Those not selected included a mathematician and programmer, an engineer, a teacher, and a stenographer and secretary.[107] Valentina Tereshkova, a weaver[108] who had also qualified as a parachuting champion, was "ideal for Khrushchev's purposes: fit, handsome, sufficiently smart for the intellectual challenges of space training, but not so advanced in her education that she could not safely represent the ordinary peasant and working classes."[109]

[107] Andrei Kislyakov. "Soviet Programme that Put First Women in Space". *The Telegraph.* 8 November 2012.
[108] Ibid.
[109] Ibid.

Tereshkova

Doran and Bizony again note that much of Soviet decision-making and response in space fight was inexorably tied to politics and public relations. Khrushchev, they explain, needed a quick and noticeable victory in the days following the Cuban Missile Crisis. It was this, they claim, that brought about his desire to "launch the kind of person no one had thought of before, a woman." Others credit the idea for the first woman in space to Korolev, who was looking for "a new first"[110] and desired to send the "message that the Soviet Union valued its citizens equally

[110] Amy Shira Teitel. Valentina Tereshkova: First Woman in Space. History of Space. *Discovery Newsletter*. June 14, 2013.

and give little girls throughout the nation the belief that they, too, could go into space someday."[111] This idea is in contrast to other historians who claimed that Korolev and other Soviets were angry that a woman had been chosen, were skeptical of her abilities, and that Korolev vowed he would not work with a female cosmonaut again after Tereshkova's difficult mission.

Tereshkova orbited earth for almost 71 hours, besting the total time of all American manned flights combined, and from space, she spoke on Moscow Radio: "Here is Seagull. I see a yellow strip. I see the earth. Everything is in order. I'm feeling fine. The machine is working well."[112] Tereshkova's flight later came under criticism for not accomplishing all of the mission goals in the areas of data collection and manual control of the craft. Some engineers reported later that Tereshkova had become ill as a result of not being able to handle the weightlessness during flight and grew more and more unable to provide ground control with the data needed.[113] Tereshkova herself disputed these claims and said she "felt no fear."[114]

Though a plan was in place for future Soviet female cosmonauts, the next Russian female did not enter space for 18 more years. Vladimir Putin extended an invitation in 2013 to Tereshkova on her 70th birthday, telling her, "Your flight was, and will remain, a matter of pride for the Soviet people, for the Russian people."[115] That same year, she offered herself for a manned mission to Mars,[116] stating, "If I had money, I would enjoy flying to Mars. This was the dream of the first cosmonauts. I wish I could realize it! I am ready to fly without coming back."[117]

The Vostok missions had clearly set the Soviet Union apart, excited its leaders and people, and upset the Americans, who still seemed to lag behind in their efforts. It is the opinion of many, however, that while the Vostoks were efforts that broke records, they were also less well-planned, being driven in many cases by Khrushchev's desire to grab headlines rather than actually moving a viable space program forward. As Peter Bond comments, "The Soviet leadership had stung the pride of the richest and most technologically advanced nation on the world, and had started a race which they could not win, at least in the short term."[118]

Chapter 6: The Voskhod Missions

In 1964, the Soviets began the Voskhod missions, apparently at the behest of Khrushchev, who was said to be impatient for another successful and headline-grabbing mission before the Americans could have success with a two-man crew.[119] Voskhod was to carry three men, including a doctor and a scientist rather than traditionally trained cosmonauts, but the increased

---

[111] Ibid.
[112] Bond, 24.
[113] "Tereshkova Celebrate Historic Flight". *The Moscow Times*. June 17, 2013.
[114] Ibid.
[115] Ibid.
[116] "First Woman in Space Dreams of Flying to Mars". Reuters. March 6, 2007.
[117] Ibid.
[118] Bond, 25.
[119] Ibid., 64.

weight of the new craft and its passengers would require that some of the safety measures from the Vostok designs would be removed, making Voskhod 1 "possibly the most dangerous mission ever."[120] As Korolev modified the Vostok capsule to fit three men instead of one, several traditional safety precautions had to go. According to Korolev's deputy, Vasily Mishin, "Fitting a crew of three people, and in spacesuits, in the cabin of the Voskhod was impossible. So- down with the spacesuits! And the cosmonauts went up without them. It was also impossible to make three hatches for evacuation. So- down with the ejection devices."[121]

---

[120] Ibid., 67.
[121] Gerard J. De Groot. *Dark Side of the Moon: The Magnificent Madness of the American Lunar Quest*. (New York: New York University Press, 2006), 189.

Voskhod 1's crew

The Voskhod's main differentiation from earlier flights was the landing procedure. Voskhod would bring its crew to the earth, with no more ejection seats or parachutes necessary. As Korolev put it, "Soviet designers have taken care to minimize loads on the human organism and the landing system ensures that when the craft touches Earth, its speed is down to zero and it lands softly."[122] Another major difference was in what the crew wore - "sky blue jackets over lightweight, dark gray suits and white helmets," rather than pressure suits.[123]

Mishin questioned the validity of Voskhod from a scientific perspective: "It was as if there was, sort of, a three-seater craft, and at the same time there wasn't. In fact, it was a circus act, for three people couldn't do any useful work in space. They were cramped just sitting! Not to mention it was dangerous to fly."[124]

While Voskhod I was in flight, there were significant developments taking place on the ground. Khrushchev was ousted from leadership, a development that later gave significance to his comment during a conversation with the Voskhod cosmonauts that a member of the Politburo was "pulling the receiver out of my hand."[125] Perhaps as a result of the political turmoil, Voskhod 1 landed, the first successful manned space landing, only about 24 hours after launch. When the crew landed, Leonid Brezhnev was the USSR's new leader.[126]

---

[122] Bond, 67.
[123] Ibid.
[124] De Groot, 189.
[125] Bond, 69.
[126] Ibid., 71.

Brezhnev

With Khrushchev's ouster, the Soviet space program lost some of its vigor and its sense of urgency diminished. Though some may argue that Khrushchev's reasons for supporting the space program were solely political and served to distract the people from his failures in agricultural and foreign policy, there can be no doubt that he "turned the USSR into an unlikely beacon of technological progress."[127] Brezhnev simply did not place as much emphasis on Soviet space feats. As Brzezinski explained, "Moscow still aimed for the moon, the ultimate bragging ground, but the effort did not have the same intensity or urgency as the past-Sputnik rush to paint the heavens red…With the milestones in space growing ever more ambitious and costly, the Kremlin's cautious new bosses preferred to spend on security rather than prestige."[128]

As a result of their frustrations with the lack of funding for manned space flights during the Brezhnev years, several cosmonauts signed a letter directed to the premier:

"Dear Leonid Ilyich!

We are writing to you to raise certain issues, which we consider very important for our state and for us. [After a brief review of Soviet space and cosmonaut history and its importance for Soviet prestige, the letter continued] …In the past year…The USA have not only caught up with us, but even surpassed us in certain areas… This lagging behind of our homeland in space exploration is especially objectionable to us, cosmonauts, but it also damages the prestige of the Soviet Union and has a negative effect on the defense efforts of the countries from the socialist camp. Why is the Soviet Union losing its leading position in space research? A common answer to this question answer is… that the USA spend on space exploration much more than does the USSR. But the matter is not only funding. The Soviet Union also allocates significant funds for space exploration. Unfortunately, in our country there are many defects in planning, organization, and management of this work. How can one speak about serious planning of space research if we do not have any plan for cosmonauts' flights?...Manned space flights are becoming more and more complex and prolonged. The preparation of such flights takes a lot of time, requires special equipment, training spacecraft, and simulators, which are now being created with huge delay and with primitive methods. To put it briefly, we need a national plan of manned space flights which would include the flight task, the date, the composition of the crew, the duration of the flight, the deadline for the preparation of a spacecraft and a simulator, and many other important issues of flight preparation.…[The letter then complains about the complicated system through which decisions must be made, resulting in a 'scattering of efforts and resources'] …Why have there not been enough ships built for our cosmonauts' flights? In any case, not because of the lack of funding. It happened because the leadership of the Missile Forces has more trust in automatic

---

[127] Brzezinski, 272.
[128] Ibid., 273.

satellites, and it underestimates the role of human beings in space research. It is a shame that in our country, which was the first to send man into outer space, for four years the question has been debated whether man is needed on board a military spacecraft. In America this question has been resolved firmly and conclusively in favor of man... We do not intend to belittle the value of automatic spacecraft. But an infatuation with them would be, at the very least, harmful. Using the Vostok and the Voskhod spacecraft, it would have been possible to carry out a large complex of very important military research and to extend the duration of flights to 10-12 days. But we have no ships, nothing on which we could fly, nothing on which we could carry out a program of space research...Dear Leonid Ilyich! We know how busy you are and nevertheless we ask you to familiarize yourself with our space affairs and needs. The 50th anniversary of the Great October [Revolution] is approaching. We would like very much to achieve new, big victories in space by the time of this great holiday..."[129]

The letter was signed by the pilot-cosmonauts of the USSR: Yuri Gagarin, Leonov, Belyaev, Titov, Nikolaev, and Bykovsky. Kamamin passed the letter on to the Minister of Defense, but it likely never made it to Brezhnev and never received a reply. Several of the cosmonauts subsequently pushed for a meeting with top government officials to further their complaint. Unfortunately for the Soviet flyers, their desire for more respect and deference coincided with a number of coming setbacks, including the death of Korolev (and a posthumous focus on the engineering and design side of the space program), the deaths of Yuri Gagarin and Komarov, and a series of launch failures after the mid-'60s. The reputation of the unflappable Soviet cosmonaut had receded, and with it any chance of political influence.[130]

Voskhod 2 was launched in March of 1965. This mission again featured an important first: the first spacewalk. The craft weighed in at almost 12,000 pounds,[131] more than 60 times heavier than Sputnik in 1957. Part of that weight came from Voskhod 2's "telescopic air lock" from which cosmonaut Alexei Leonov became the first man to experience space outside of a vehicle. Leonov was tethered to the Voskhod capsule, but otherwise floated freely in space after announcing to his comrade still in the capsule, "I'm pushing off! Man has walked out into space!"[132] Leonov experienced some difficulty upon reentering the capsule when the spacewalk was complete as his suit had expanded in space and he was now too wide to re-enter the narrow hatch and air lock. Fortunately, he was able to release some of the pressure from his suit and re-renter the capsule, albeit with difficulty.[133] Voskhod 2 also required the cosmonauts to manually

[129] "Soviet Cosmonauts' Letter to Leonid Brezhnev", October 22, 1965
    <http://web.mit.edu/slava/space/documents/brezhnev-letter.htm>
[130] James T. Andrews and Asif Siddiqi. *Into the Cosmos: Space Exploration and Soviet Culture.* (Pittsburgh: University of Pittsburgh Press, 2011), 99-100.
[131] Von Braun, Ordway III, and Dooling. 203.
[132] Ibid., 77.
[133] De Groot, 193.

fire their landing rockets to knock themselves out of orbit, as the retro-rockets designed for that purpose failed. This allowed them to return to Earth, but it was a difficult reentry that resulted in their landing in trees in the Siberian forest. The retrieval of the cosmonauts took over 48 hours.[134]

Sergei Korolev, the person responsible for so many achievements throughout the 1950s and 1960s, died after a failed surgery in 1966. Korolev had received a thorough examination at the Kremlin's medical center, where he was declared in very good health. In fact, William E. Burrows recounts the story of Korolev being told he had another 20 years to expect of a long and healthy life. A slightly bleeding polyp in Korolev's colon, however, was scheduled to be removed, and during what should have been routine surgery, Korolev began bleeding uncontrollably. Moreover, an additional large tumor was found in his abdomen. As a result of the bleeding and strain on Korolev's heart, he died on the operating table.[135] Brian Harvey claims that with Korolev's death, the Soviet space program was severely undermined, crediting Korolev with the ability and drive to carry out so many Soviet space achievements along with his political cohort, Khrushchev.[136]

The death of Korolev and his vision, as well as the tragedy of America's Apollo I fire and the death of three American astronauts on January 27, 1967, shook the space community and later elicited the following remarks from the head of cosmonaut training, General Kamanin: "We must be fully convinced, however, that the fight will be a success. The flights we are preparing will be more complicated than the previous ones, and thus preparation for them will have to be appropriately longer. We do not intend to speed up our programme. Excessive haste leads to fatal accidents, as in the case of the tragic deaths of three American astronauts last January."

Chapter 7: The Soyuz Program

The caution the Soviets had promised was in question when they launched Soyuz, the Soviet's first manned mission since Voskhod 2.[137] Soyuz I had was supposed to be the fulfillment of a long-awaited multiple-manned mission, but when it launched in April of 1967, only one cosmonaut, Vladimir Komarov, was on board.[138] The Soviets had been unusually reticent about the purposes of this flight, but many suspected that Soyuz would rendezvous with another craft to be launched in the day following and complete a docking and exchange mission.[139] In fact, the name Soyuz means union in Russian.[140]

---

[134] Ibid.
[135] Burrows.
[136] Harvey, 8.
[137] Von Braun, Ordway III, and Dooling, 205.
[138] Bond, 144.
[139] Ibid., 145.
[140] Shepard and Slayton, 217.

Komarov

What happened instead would be a matter of controversy for years to come. After its initial orbit, Soyuz developed problems; the craft had been designed with two solar panels which would allow for Soyuz to draw power from the sun rather than a battery, but only one of the panels opened, which meant that the systems were operating with only half of the power intended.[141] An attempt to use other systems to generate enough electricity to open the second panel failed, and the Soyuz developed communication problems as well. Between the 7th and 13th orbits, Soyuz would have no communication with ground control and Komarov was directed to "try to get some sleep."[142] When contact was re-established at the 17th orbit, Soyuz was "out of control," according to the Soviet flight control director. "The spacecraft is going into tumbles that the pilot has difficulty controlling. We must face the truth. He might not survive re-entry."[143]

At that point, it was decided that the second launch would be canceled and the rest of the mission aborted, and though Komarov did an admirable job of bringing Soyuz back under control for re-entry, the extreme speed with which it entered the atmosphere caused the two chutes that Komarov deployed to become twisted and useless in slowing the craft down. Soyuz impacted the Earth at 400 miles per hour, and Komarov's body was recovered in the ashes.[144]

The Soyuz mission remains a point of controversy. Many say that Komarov went into space knowing that the Soyuz was unready and agreed to the mission only to save his backup cosmonaut and friend, Yuri Gagarin, who had discovered over 200 structural problems with the craft and recommended that the mission be postponed.[145] According to testimony of those listening to transmissions in nearby Turkey, Komarov died "cursing the people who had put him inside a botched spaceship."[146] While that is considered by many to be an apocryphal story, there's no doubt Komarov must've had those kinds of thoughts running through his mind as he met his end.

The Soviets continued the development of Soyuz, making changes that allowed them to launch Soyuz 2 (unmanned) in October of 1968 and Soyuz 3, a manned flight, only a day later.[147]

Chapter 8: The Program's Legacy

When it started becoming clear to the Soviets that they might lose the race for a manned mission to the moon, Soviet political leaders encouraged designers and engineers to compete with one another for alternative firsts. Failures were to be kept as quiet as possible, and successes broadcast as great Soviet victories. The Zond and Venera missions aimed for landings on Mars and Venus respectively, and while more than 20 of these attempts failed, the Soviets were eventually successful in at least crash landing a craft onto both planets.[148]

There can be no doubt that the Soviet space program had begun to decline in its accomplishments in the late '60s as funding mechanisms slowed, the United States successfully

---

[141] Ibid. 218.
[142] Ibid.
[143] Ibid., 219.
[144] Burrows, 413.
[145] Robert Krulwich. "Cosmonaut Crashed Into Earth 'Crying In Rage'" NPR.org March 18, 2011
[146] Ibid.
[147] Von Braun, Ordway III, and Dooling, 205.
[148] Burrows, 461.

landed a man on the moon, and program failures brought the height of former Soviet space glory to an end. Authors James T. Andrews and Asif A. Siddiqi offer dual explanations for the communist party's interest in a space program. Though the first is simply the Marxist desire for power and reshaping, another explanation "derived from the Bolshevik's own vision to remake Russia into a modern state, one that would compare and compete with the leading capitalist nations in forging a new path to the future."[149]

Whatever the ultimate goal, the Soviet space program enhanced the reputation of the Soviet system in the eyes of much of the world, kept pressure on the United States, and provided millions of Soviet citizens a sense of pride and accomplishment. Dora and Bizony note the rarity of individual glory in Soviet life and cultural history, and point out how the legacy of the space program breaks that rule, with men like Gagarin recalled "with genuine affection a peasant boy with a winning smile" and manned space flight itself being a win against the Americans, who arrived late in popular eyes.[150]

Russia's celebration of Gagarin's accomplishments included the 1975 Gagarin march that commemorated Vostock I's accomplishment. The song's lyrics were spliced with recordings of Gagarin's transmissions to earth:

"This is Moscow

This is Moscow calling

On the 12th of April, the Soviet Union orbited a spaceship around the Earth with a man on board

The astronaut is a Soviet citizen: Major Gagarin, Yuri Alekseyevich

The World's first cosmonaut

The first to open the door into the unknown

The first to step over the threshold of our homeland

The whole planet knew him and loved him

Gagarin...

Was it hazardous? Yes, it was

The first strides into the unknown were about to be made

---

[149] Andrews and Siddiqi.
[150] Doran and Bizony, 2.

The hero who blazed the trail for the stars

Every one of us was with Yuri Gagarin as he orbited the Earth 190 miles above us.

Astronaut to Earth: I can see forests, rivers, [?] all around

Everything's so beautiful, it's wonderful, it's wonderful...

The whole planet knew him and loved him."

A Soviet propaganda poster of the early '60s features a red hand, outstretched to the sky and sending off a red rocket marked "CCCP." The proud poster reminded each citizen who watched the skies in hope of the next event, "Soviet man—be proud, you opened the road to stars from Earth!" "Glory to the conquerors of the universe!"[151]

Online Resources

Other titles about 20th century history by Charles River Editors

Other titles about the Space Race on Amazon

Bibliography

Andrews, James T. and Asif A. Siddiqi, Ed. *Into the Cosmos: Space Exploration and Soviet Culture.* Pittsburgh: University of Pittsburgh Press, 2011.

Bond, Peter. *Heroes in Space: From Gagarin to Challenger.* Basil Blackwell Inc., 1987.

Brzezinski, Matthew. *Red Moon Rising.* New York: Henry Holt and Company, 2007.

Burgess, Colin and Chris Dubbs. *Animals in Space: From Research Rockets to the Space Shuttle.* Springer Science and Business Media, 2007.

Burrows, William E. *The New Ocean: The Story of the First Space Age.* New York: Random House, 1998.

Cassutt, Michael. "Star City at 50". Air and Space Magazine. *Smithsonian.* March 2011.

De Groot, Gerard J. *Dark Side of the Moon: The Magnificent Madness of the American Lunar Quest.* New York: New York University Press, 2006.

---

[151] Laura Stampler. "These Soviet Space-Race Propaganda Posters Retain Their Delusional Intensity 50 Years Later." Business Insider. April 26, 2012.

Dickson, Paul. *Sputnik: The Shock of a Century*. Bloomsbury Publishing, 2009.

Divine, Robert A. *The Sputnik Challenge*. Oxford University Press, 1993.

Doran, Jamie and Piers Bizony. *Starman: The Truth Behind the Legend of Yuri Gagarin*. New York: Walker Publishing Company. 2011.

Erickson, Lance K. *Space Flight: History, Technology, and Operations*. Roman and Littlefield, 2010.

-----"First Woman in Space Dreams of Flying to Mars". Reuters. March 6, 2007.

Hall, Rex, Shayler David, and Bert Vis. *Russian Cosmonauts: Inside the Yuri Gagarin Training Center*. Springer Science & Business Media, Oct 5, 2007.

Hardesty, Von and Gene Eisman. *Epic Rivalry: The inside Story of the Soviet and American Space Race*. Washington, D.C.: National Geographic, 2007.

Harvey, Brian and Olga Zakutnyaya. "Russian Space Probes: Scientific Discoveries and Future Missions." Springer Science & Business Media, May 4, 2011.

Hopkinson, Harry. *Bluff of the Century: Sputnik and the Cold War*.

Kislyakov, Andrei. "Soviet Programme That Put First Women in Space". *The Telegraph*. 8 November 2012.

----- "Konstantin E. Tsiolkovsky." *NASA*. September 22, 2010.

Krulwich, Robert. "Cosmonaut Crashed Into Earth 'Crying In Rage'" *NPR.org*. March 18, 2011

Leonov, Alexei and David Scott. *Two Sides of the Moon: Our Story of the Cold War Space Race*. New York: Thomas Dunne Books, 2006.

Mahoney, John. "Fifty Years Later, Looking Back at the Dawn of the Space Race". *Popular Science Magazine*, October 4, 2007.

Marcus, Edwin. "Awake At Last?" Library of Congress Prints and Photographs Division. Washington, D.C. 1957.

Osborn, Andrew. Yuri Gagarin Death Mystery Solved after Forty Years. *The Telegraph*. 8 January, 2010.

Rodgers, Paul R. "Yuri Gagarin: The Man Who Fell to Earth." *The Independent*. April 3, 2011.

-----"Some Reactions Overseas". *Life Magazine*. Vol. 50, No. 16. April 21, 1961.

----"Soviet Cosmonauts' Letter to Leonid Brezhnev", October 22, 1965
<http://web.mit.edu/slava/space/documents/brezhnev-letter.htm>

------"Soviet Moon Lander Discovered Water on the Moon in 1976." *MIT Technology Review.* May 30, 2012.

-----"Soviet Traveler Returns From Out of This World". *Life Magazine.* Vol. 50, No. 16. April 21, 1961.

Stampler, Laura. "These Soviet Space-Race Propaganda Posters Retain Their Delusional Intensity 50 Years Later." *Business Insider.* April 26, 2012

Teitel, Amy Shira. "Valentina Tereshkova: First Woman in Space." History of Space. *Discovery Newsletter.* June 14, 2013.

----"Tereshkova Celebrate Historic Flight". *The Moscow Times.* June 17, 2013.

Tyson, Neil deGrasse. *Space Chronicles: Facing the Ultimate Frontier.* New York: W.W. Norton and Company, 2012.

Von Braun, Wernher, Frederick I. Ordway III, and Dave Dooling. *Space Travel: A History.* New York: Harper and Row, 1985.

Wainwright, Oliver. "The Dogs that Conquered Space." *The Guardian.* September 2, 2014.

-----YU.A. Gagarin Research and Test Cosmonaut Training Center. "GCTC History". *Russian Federal Space Agency.*

21307974R00033

Printed in Great Britain
by Amazon